'Evening wheat field abstract'
Oil on board
107 x 122 cm
(See page 39)

'Evening wheat field abstract'
Detail, actual size

'Wittenham Clumps left abstract'
Oil on board
122 x 107 cm
(See page 31)

'Wittenham Clumps left abstract'
Detail, actual size

'Dark field left abstract'
Oil on board
122 x 107 cm
(See page 33)

'Dark field left abstract'
Detail, actual size

'Bright trees abstract'
Oil on board
122 x 107 cm
(See page 37)

'Bright trees abstract'
Detail, actual size

'Ploughed fields abstract'
Oil on board
122 x 107 cm
(See page 41)

'Ploughed fields abstract'
Detail, actual size

17

'Dark field right abstract'
Oil on board
122 x 107 cm
(See page 33)

'Dark field right abstract'
Detail, actual size

15

'Wittenham Clumps foreground abstract'
Oil on board
122 x 107 cm
(See page 31)

'Wittenham Clumps foreground abstract'
Detail, actual size

'Into the wheat abstract'
Oil on board
107 x 122 cm
(See page 29)

'Into the wheat abstract'
Detail, actual size

11

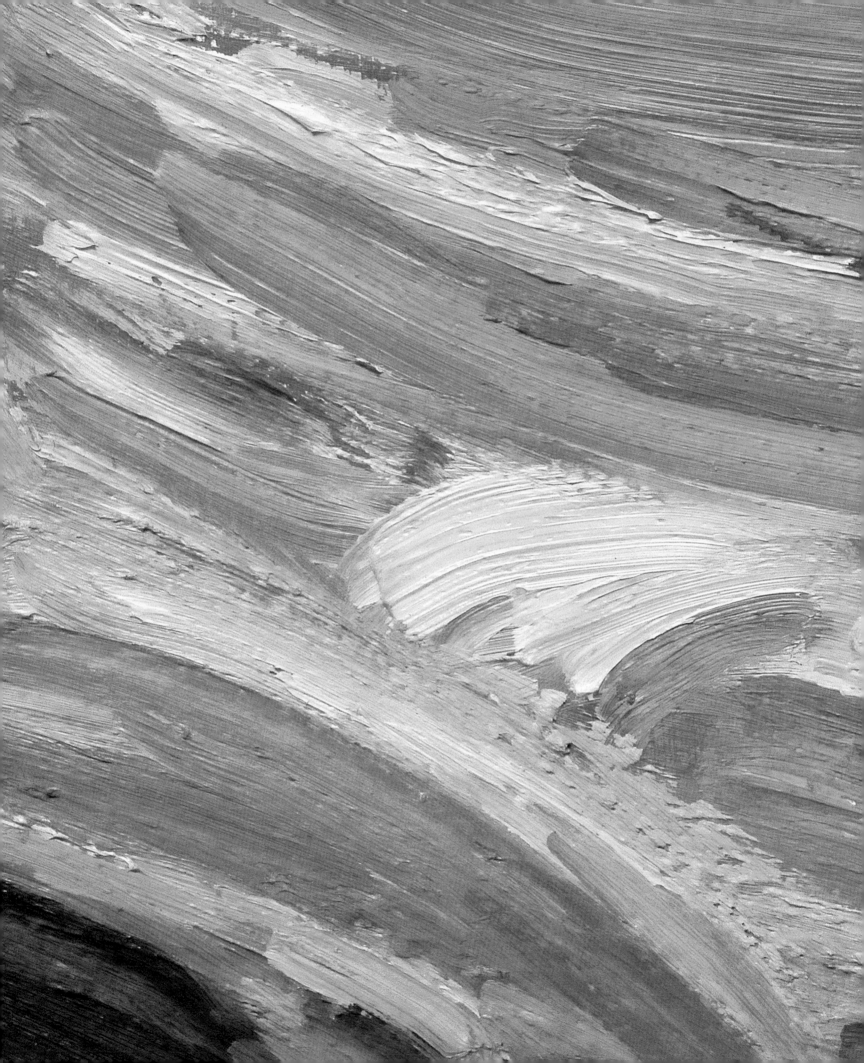

'Inside beech copse abstract'
Oil on board
122 x 107 cm

'Inside beech copse abstract'
Detail, actual size

printed it out on an A4 sheet of paper. This gives me a larger reference to work from when at the easel. One consequence of this operation is that my printer often produces a quite different version of the colours which seem more attractive than the original.

As the large abstract is not an enlarged facsimile of the original I feel free to take advantage of these accidents. After all, making use of accidents in the course of painting is, for me, an essential part of painting. In fact the whole idea of using

the possibly unconscious mark-making found in a representative picture as well as the accidents of the A4 sheet printing, doubles the chance of accidents happening.

Finally, the detail from the large abstracts included in the catalogue suggest a further way to explore.

The pictures in the exhibition are not necessarily hung in the same manner as they appear in this catalogue.

Nick Schlee 2017

'Inside beech copse'
Oil on board
102 x 82 cm

ABSTRACTIONS

I never really did trust abstract pictures. Thy were often seductive in their colour and composition. But they played on my senses without revealing exactly where they were coming from. Like some music, they did not have a 'story line' that would help me navigate my senses safely through the colour and lines, tones and textures that were their armoury of attack.

I am the sort of artist that likes to meet his viewers half way. I paint recognisable landscapes that I hope will convey my own excited response to what I see in nature.

But I have always recognised that very often my realistic paintings often toppled over into abstract shapes. The two vocabularies were identical. The balancing act between interpreting paint marks as representational or abstract gave the picture a dangerous excitement and an extra dimension.

Then I observed from a recent catalogue of my paintings that the full page, same size details taken from a representative painting shown on the opposite page were extremely powerful images. Bereft of their surrounding context they did indeed appear abstract.

This exhibition shows ten such 'abstracts' abstracted from original representational landscape picture writ large.

I have selected portions of the painting that when seen in close up seem to have powerful brushstrokes, rhythm and pattern that qualify them for becoming the subject of a large canvas. Sometimes I have turned them on their side to deny the viewer the possibility of seeing too readily the reality from which they were derived. Even, in some cases, the colour or tones have been altered to enhance their attraction.

The large paintings are shown together with the smaller original source paintings. The fact that I know that the marks I made in the the first painting are representative imparts them with a legitimacy in my eyes. Knowing their provenance gives me the confidence to exploit their character on an imposing scale

But I find that however attractive the detail looks in terms of paint, colour and texture these are difficult for me to reproduce accurately on the larger picture. In fact I have had to forego the luscious thickness of brushstroke seen in close up for something else. So because of the practical difficulties I have used brushstrokes and quality of paint that I hope are attractive in their own right. I have attempted to retain the colour, shapes and directional thrust suggested by the original strokes and colour.

Again, for practical reasons, I have photographed the original detail and

Contents

First published in Great Britain in 2017 by
Academy Press, 23 College Road, Brighton BN2 1JB

Copyright © 2017 Nick Schlee

ISBN 978-0-9558923-3-2

Front Cover: *'Into the wheat abstract' (detail)*,
Oil on board, Page 11

Dimensions given in centimetres, height before width.

Designed by Academy Press
Artwork by The Graphics Room
Photography by Geoff Fletcher

Printed in Northern Ireland by
Nicholson and Bass Ltd.

Further copies of this book can be obtained
from Academy Press
jemimaschlee@gmail.com

Other books available in the series include:

Nick Schlee Drawing to painting
Nick Schlee Drawings from 1958 - 2010
Nick Schlee Paintings from 1987 - 2008

www.nickschlee.co.uk

Nick Schlee
Abstractions

ap Academy Press

'Inside beech copse' Detail, Oil on board. (Page 7)

Nick Schlee
Abstractions

GROUP EXHIBITIONS

1988 Sue Rankin Gallery, London
1990 Roy Miles Gallery, London
1991 University College, Oxford
1992 Art '92, London
      20th Century British Art, London
1993 Museum of Modern Art, Oxford
      City Gallery, Leicester
1994 Templeton College, Oxford
1995 Arts Centre, Nottingham University
      Midlands Art Centre, Birmingham
1997 Beatrice Royal Gallery, Hampshire
1998 CCA Gallery, Oxford
2013 St. Barbe Museum, Hampshire
2014 Gerald Moore gallery, London
2016 St. Barbe Museum, Hampshire
2017 Southampton City Art Gallery

PUBLIC COLLECTIONS

City of London Guildhall Gallery
Gallery Oldham
Hampshire County Council
John Creasey Museum, Salisbury
Liverpool University
National Trust
Oxfordshire Museums
Portsmouth University
Reading Museum and Art Gallery
River & Rowing Museum, Henley
Southampton City Art Gallery
Swindon Museum and Art Gallery
Wessex Collection, Longleat House
West Berkshire Museum
Wiltshire Heritage Museum

NICK SCHLEE BIOGRAPHY

1931 Born in Weybridge, Surrey, England

1947 Won both Gold and Silver medals
for under 18s given by the Royal
Drawing Society

1955 Studied part time at the Art Students
League, New York

1957 Lived in London. Studied part-time at the
Central School, Morely College, Putney
Art School and the Slade. Exhibited at
various ILEA exhibitions, The Spirit of
London and the Royal Academy

1989 Lives and works in Upper Basildon,
Berkshire

ONE MAN EXHIBITIONS

1987 Yehudi Menuhin School, Sussex

1988 The Grange, Rottingdean

1990 Wantage Museum, Oxford

1992 Flying Colours Gallery, Edinburgh

1993 Castlegate House Gallery, Cumbria

1994 Barbican Centre, London

1995 Wantage Museum, Oxfordshire

1996 Simon Carter Gallery, Suffolk
The University of Liverpool
Christ Church Picture Gallery, Oxford

1998 Gallery 27, London

2000 Gallery 27, London

2001 Corn Exchange, Newbury

2002 Gallery 27, London
River & Rowing Museum, Henley

2003 Christ Church Picture Gallery, Oxford

2004 Modern Artists Gallery, Oxfordshire
Gallery 27, London

2006 Oxford Said Business School
Corn Exchange, Newbury
Gallery 27, London

2008 West Berkshire Museum
Modern Artists Gallery, Oxfordshire
Gallery 27, London

2010 River & Rowing Museum, Henley
Gallery 27, London

2012 Wiltshire Heritage Museum
Modern Artists Gallery, Oxfordshire
Gallery 27, London

2013 Basildon Park, National Trust

2014 Gallery 8, London

2015 54, The Gallery, London
Gallery 8, London

2016 Modern Artists Gallery, Oxfordshire

2017 Arlington Arts Centre, Newbury
Oxfordshire County Museum

2018 Christ Church Picture Gallery, Oxford
Gallery 8, London

'Evening wheat field'
Oil pastel
30 x 40 cm

'Ploughed fields'
Oil pastel
21 x 29 cm

'Field edge'
Oil pastel
30 x 40 cm

'Bright trees'
Oil pastel
30 x 40 cm

'Wittenham Clumps'
Oil pastel
21 x 29 cm

'Dark field'
Oil pastel
21 x 29 cm

'Inside beech copse'
Oil pastel
40 x 30 cm

'Into the wheat'
Oil pastel
30 x 40 cm

'Ploughed fields'
Oil on board
60 x 74 cm

'Ploughed fields' Detail

'Evening wheat field'
Oil on board
80 x 102 cm

'Evening wheat field' Detail

'Bright trees'
Oil on board
60 x 74 cm

'Bright trees' Detail

'Field edge'
Oil on board
60 x 74 cm

'Field edge' Detail

'*Dark field*'
Oil on board
60 x 74 cm

'Dark field' Detail left

'Dark field' Detail right

'Wittenham Clumps'
Oil on board
60 x 74 cm

'Wittenham Clumps' Detail left

'Wittenham Clumps' Detail foreground

30

'Into the wheat'
Oil on board
60 x 74 cm

'Into the wheat' Detail

Field edge abstract'
Oil on board
122 x 107 cm
(See page 35)

'Field edge abstract'
Detail, actual size